The Twelve Degrees of Silence

Original translation from the French by Françoise Reuter and Lucinda M. Vardey. Additional reflections by Lucinda M. Vardey. Copyright © 2012 Novalis Publishing Inc., Toronto, Canada. All rights reserved. Sale authorised in the United Kingdom and Europe.

Published by
The Bible Reading Fellowship
15 The Chambers, Vineyard
Abingdon OX14 3FE
United Kingdom
Tel: +44 (0)1865 319700
Email: enquiries@brf.org.uk
Website: www.brf.org.uk
BRF is a Registered Charity

ISBN 978 0 85746 407 1
First published 2014 by Novalis Publishing, Toronto, Canada
UK edition first published 2015
10 9 8 7 6 5 4 3 2 1 0

All rights reserved

Acknowledgements
Unless otherwise stated, scripture quotations are taken from The New Revised Standard Version of the Bible, Anglicised edition, copyright © 1989, 1995 by the Division of Christian Education of the National Council of the Churches of Christ in the United States of America. Used by permission. All rights reserved.

Cover image: Jeff Saward/Labyrinthos

A catalogue record for this book is available from the British Library

Printed and bound by CPI Group (UK) Ltd, Croydon CR0 4YY

The Twelve Degrees of Silence

Marie-Aimée de Jésus OCD

Edited with Introductions and Reflections
by Lucinda M. Vardey

Translated by Françoise Reuter and Lucinda M. Vardey

*Dedicated with gratitude to
Marie-Aimée de Jésus
and
Saint John of the Cross*

Contents

Preface 7

Introducing the life and work
of Marie-Aimée de Jésus 9

Praying the Twelve Degrees of Silence 23

The Twelve Degrees of Silence by Marie-Aimée de Jésus
(additional reflections by Lucinda M. Vardey) 27

Afterword 73

Notes 75

*Silence is not the absence of sounds,
but something infinitely more real than sounds
and the centre of a harmony more perfect
than anything which a combination of sounds can produce.
Furthermore, there are degrees of silence.
There is a silence in the beauty of the universe
which is like a noise when compared with the
silence of God.*[1]

Preface

Silence has always woven its wisdom around a solitary hermit's cave and through the cells and loggias of cloisters. Hidden delicately under the rough cloth of religious habits, this wordless prayer has revealed the graces of divine love, purity of heart, strength of soul, clarity of mind and a freedom that can be expressed only by joy. Yet, all these gifts of silence are not beyond reach for those still living in the world. Today, more than ever, there is a thirst for finding peace amid the busyness of daily life, and a longing to discover a way of prayer that can become a contemplative practice in which to grow inwardly and mature spiritually. Our cloister can be our home, our silent corner, a haven to sit—like Martha's sister, Mary—at Jesus' feet, to listen intently to what he desires to speak to our hearts.

The practice of listening in prayer requires discipline and direction. To truly hear the Lord's voice, we need to prepare. Preparation helps us recognise the hindrances, the roadblocks we place in the way—the inner voices of contradiction, the 'to do's, the worries, how we allow others' ways to affect our own. We need simply to understand ourselves as we are and be complete in that understanding, mindless of exterior influences. We need to be intimate with the truth of ourselves that lies behind the door to our hearts where Jesus stands knocking to enter.[2]

This little book contains the wisdom of a 19th-century French Carmelite nun, Sister Marie-Aimée de Jésus, who was drawn to listen deeply to the sounds of silence and allow them to direct her on her way to giving all to God. Desiring only 'perfection', she strove towards the riches and light of God that purified her into a state of enduring surrender and, eventually, divine union. She thereby reached the eternal shore, a place where her soul lived more fully than her physical being, and from there she abandoned herself into the abundant torrent of God's grace and love.

The call to relinquish what keeps us apart from God is common to all, as is Jesus' promise of abiding love and truth. Marie-Aimée de Jésus' twelve degrees of silence offer the means through which we can transform what Edith Stein (Saint Teresa Benedicta of the Cross) explained was our sensory selves while keeping 'in step with the rise of the spiritual human being'.[3] By following what Marie-Aimée de Jésus prescribed, we can evolve through the shedding of what can be false, superfluous and unnecessary, while developing and growing in the fruits of virtue and divine intimacy. Silence directs us away from only *doing for* God, and towards *being with* God. Silence pulls us along, slowly and surely, to its ultimate aim: the peace and selfless joy of abiding solely *in* God.[4]

The more interior is the soul, the more secure, substantial and delightful; because the more interior it is, the purer it is. And the greater the purity, the more abundantly, frequently, and generously God communicates himself.

SAINT JOHN OF THE CROSS[5]

Introducing the life and work of Marie-Aimée de Jésus (1839–74)

BACKGROUND AND BIOGRAPHY[6]

All Christian mysticism is propelled by love and the desire for inner perfection. Many of the works of Christian mystics detail the course of interior scrutiny, which involves not only the purifying of one's soul but also the development of virtue to be ready for divine union. A few of our well-known women saints documented the route of their journey with methods and imagery to help define the way. For instance, Saint Teresa of Avila used the rooms of a castle, Saint Clare of Assisi, a mirror, Saint Catherine of Siena, a bridge, and Saint Thérèse of Lisieux, a flower. Sister Marie-Aimée de Jésus introduces another way, a way that unfurls by degrees within an envelope of silence. Known by only a few, this woman was brought to wider attention through the writings of Edith Stein.

A successful philosopher, feminist thinker and lecturer, Edith Stein was called to a Carmelite vocation after reading Saint Teresa of Avila's autobiography. During her eight years as a religious, Edith wrote essays and translated writings by Saint John of the Cross. Part of the tradition of Carmel is to circulate among the communities stories of the lives, examples and spiritual virtues of other Carmelites. Edith was particularly gifted in this area. She wrote with deep comprehension of the beauty of mystical life, of the love and attention of souls turned towards unity with Jesus, their bridegroom. One of her essays was on a French sister, Marie-Aimée de Jésus (1839–74). The convent where Marie-Aimée resided (originally in Paris, now in Créteil) had published a book of Marie-Aimée's writings in 1922 under the title

A Chosen Vessel of Divine Wisdom. A German edition of her work, *Die zwölf Grade des Schweigens* (*The Twelve Degrees of Silence*), appeared in 1937. Two years later, in 1939, Edith submitted her essay on Marie-Aimée's life and work to her prioress at the Carmel in Echt, the Netherlands.

Identifying Marie-Aimée's life's pilgrimage as a way of the cross, which Edith herself was to eventually walk, she exposed its essential nature. In her last work, published as *The Science of the Cross*, Edith quoted the fourth-century Bishop of Milan, Saint Ambrose, on the essence of such a journey—one that leads to total denial of self 'interiorly as well as exteriorly' and 'death' to self in every respect. 'Whoever schools himself in this will achieve and find all and more than that.'[7]

By using Jesus' life and sufferings as a prism, Edith chose to divide her essay on Marie-Aimée into the following sections: Bethlehem, Nazareth, The Desert, The Task, and It Is Finished.

In an introduction to volume XI of Edith Stein's *Complete Works* (in which this particular essay appeared), it was suggested that Marie-Aimée's depth of wisdom and disciplined mental attitudes on the path of perfection of the soul were where Edith's own convictions, knowledge and understanding found fellowship. By encountering Marie-Aimée's personal journey of faith, Edith recognised her own. Such an intrinsic spiritual friendship was made only a few years before Edith met her death at Auschwitz in 1942.

Marie-Aimée de Jésus was a natural mystic. With little formal education, she managed to express in honest, sparse and poetic language the steps she experienced to loving union, providing a method, a formational discipline of silence unique in Christian literature. Silence plays an essential part in the life of a Carmelite, and Marie-Aimée had an inherent love for it, a penchant for its qualities, a comprehension of its power and an embrace of its infallibility as her soul's exclusive companion. Her arrival at this realisation came after much childhood poverty, upheaval and loss, but Edith pointed to Marie-Aimée's religious name—which means 'loved by Jesus'—as the secret of her life from the beginning.

Dorothée Quoniam was born on the feast of the Holy Name of Jesus, 14 January 1839, in a thatched hut in Le Rozel, a village in Normandy. Edith likened this simple abode to the stable at Bethlehem. Dorothée's father, who worked as a gardener, struggled to provide enough for his family. Both he and his wife were devout people. Dorothée's mother, although unable to read or write with any proficiency, knew some of the stories of the lives of the saints and imparted much 'heavenly wisdom' to her family—so much so that Dorothée felt quite at home in the celestial spheres from an early age. When she was four, she heard her mother utter the word 'Almighty' in reference to God and began to repeat it to herself as a prayer. This resulted in an invitation to betrothal from her beloved Lord; she would eventually become his bride. Edith explained that this betrothal was 'to the crucifix', because Dorothée was to walk the path of suffering.

The first step on this path came when her family was forced to move from their country home to Paris, at the suggestion of an uncle. Dorothée's forfeiting of the freedom of the fields for confinement in an attic apartment was very difficult. She wrote that as a child, she found nothing of satisfaction except the beauty of the natural world, in which she relished what her mother had taught her was 'God's composition'. However, living in the close quarters of an apartment made her mother notice the special graces in her daughter, 'this elect soul', which she resolved to support. She sent six-year-old Dorothée into the care of the Sisters of Charity (Vincentians) as a day pupil in the Parish of Saint Roch. There, Dorothée made friends easily, and many wanted to spend as much time as they could in her company. Her popularity spread among the young and the old, and she took every opportunity to talk about God.

Dorothée's sufferings were multiplied by the inflictions of fears and assaults in her spirit from 'the enemy of all goodness' when her family became so destitute that they had to rely on social assistance and handouts from friends. Even such support was not enough to save three of Dorothée's siblings. Soon after, her mother also died, leaving her young but capable daughter in charge of the household tasks. Dorothée, now nine years old, was forced to leave school and step into her mother's shoes. Edith noted that all these occurrences were 'full of fruitful seeds for the future'.

While adoption by a relative seemed a natural consequence, Dorothée's mother had specified her desire for her daughter before her own death. The girl was to be placed in the orphanage run by the Sisters of Charity. Dorothée was not to return, as she had hoped, to her previous school, but instead went to live in a house for children with special needs. A month later, her father died, followed by her younger sister; after her eldest brother fell ill and died at the age of 18, Dorothée became her family's sole survivor. Even with the losses she endured, she found much joy at her first Holy Communion, a joy that would grow with every Eucharist.

While she possessed a demeanour of 'gentleness and goodness', her interior life took many tumultuous turns. Her practice of 'severe acts of self-denial' was not enough to distract her from earthly temptations, which led to a period where she abstained from the Eucharist. This was remedied after the Lord invited her back. Edith wrote, 'He took possession of her heart anew and locked it for ever against everything other than himself.' Jesus was to reveal himself to Dorothée in human form on many occasions, and as she grew, he also grew within these revelations, as if 'he seemed to grow up with her'.

In one incident, when Dorothée's relatives had arranged a meeting with a suitor, Jesus appeared to her beside the young man and said, 'Compare!' Her destiny, which was clearly set, made all attempts at matchmaking futile.

In 1857, the two orphanages merged into one new building, which caused much upheaval among the sisters and teachers, many of whom were transferred. During this time of transition, Dorothée's role was as peacemaker and bridge builder, which brought her to the attention of the superior, Sister Eugénie Michelin. But Dorothée's sufferings continued when her newfound friend, a young nun called Sister Louise Rousseille, died within a year of their meeting.

As far as her interior progress was concerned, Dorothée presumed that the mystical capacities with which she was endowed were normal to everyone, and, as no one spoke of them, she thought it was usual to remain silent. But when a biography of Teresa of Avila fell into her hands, she took the saint's advice about the need for a priest as confidant and confessor. After praying for guidance, she confided in Father

Gamard SJ, a priest with much experience, who had led a retreat for the pupils. This encounter established their lifelong relationship. Dorothée had known about Saint Teresa from a book her mother had given her as a child. She recalled that 'her soul was unaware then that the Divine's seed had been planted in her heart'. Now she identified even more with the saint, wanting to step on to her way of perfection. 'This is my way to heaven,' she wrote. 'Teresa lives and dies holy, I also want to live and die holy.'

Now 17, Dorothée had completed her responsibilities at the orphanage and, with the support of her superiors, was free to pursue a Carmelite novitiate. The obvious convent to approach was near the orphanage on West Street, but, after taking a walk one day, Dorothée happened upon the Carmel of the Avenue de Saxe and heard the words, 'This is where I want you.' The prioress was encouraging but was concerned about Dorothée's fragile health and lack of means. Yet Dorothée knew that, after considering all the alternative orders, she wanted the prayer and solitude that Carmel offered. During her discernment she wrote:

Each has its fame, but I humbly pass by the one famed for its learning, reverently bow before the one known for its silence. I strike my breast when I pass the one famed for its penance, am enthusiastic about the one known for its poverty. However, I rush toward the one that has above all glories, the incomparable glory of love.

The newly elected prioress of the chosen Carmel, Mother Sophie of Saint Elijah, heard Sister Eugénie Michelin's petitions on behalf of her pupil, and, after the procurement of a small dowry (received from Dorothée's uncle), accepted her on 27 August 1859. Mother Sophie was described as a 'true mother, as good as she was firm, full of understanding and with a reverence for extraordinary graces', even though she herself had not been gifted in this area. The novice mistress, Sister Isabelle of the Nativity, however, was not as inclined to such things, possessing a more fearful disposition that prevented Dorothée from confiding her innermost spiritual experiences and revelations. This caution caused Sister Isabelle to become suspicious and malicious towards the new postulant. But Father Gamard, who was the confessor to the monastery, recognised the 'specially graced child' and became her stalwart supporter through 'the trials of her thorny ascent'.

The prayer life of the convent (seven hours a day), plus the solitude and silence, suited Dorothée's deepest inclinations. At one time, she was noticed by a sister, standing and listening in her cell during the midday silence; later, when asked about what she had been doing, she replied, 'Listening to the silence.' This incident bred what Edith Stein called 'the wonderfully deep little paper' on the Twelve Degrees of Silence.

Dorothée's clothing celebration took place on 15 February 1860, after further concerns for her health were overcome, but her admission to profession a year later was again questioned due to her physical weakness. While the sisters gathered in Chapter to decide, Dorothée had a vision of her mother pleading with the Trinity to have mercy on her daughter. When her mother turned to Dorothée with a smile, the novice mistress brought the good news of her acceptance. Just before the official day of admission, 18 April 1860, Dorothée received a vision of Jesus' heavenly beauty, and on the day of admission itself the Lord 'instructed her in how he wanted to be loved by her'. During the ceremony, she saw the Holy Trinity, and then the Son of God bent down towards her and took her as his bride. The little girl who had become betrothed at the age of four had finally received her spousal blessing.

Edith described Sister Marie-Aimée de Jésus as having 'a delicate face of angelic purity and spirituality, big, soft and deeply penetrating eyes' that carried in them a combined knowledge of the natural and supernatural. Her 'entire nature breathed God's presence' and she was 'inexhaustible in demonstrating sisterly love', to the point that she was once placed under suspicion for 'inappropriate attraction' towards a sister she was helping on the way to perfection.

Marie-Aimée's talent as a writer of the experiences of inner life began when she took up her pen in defence of her Lord after the popular publication in 1863 of a book by Renan, *The Life of Jesus*, in which Christ's divinity was questioned. Marie-Aimée felt a compunction to break her beloved silence to offer proof that Jesus was indeed the Son of God. She embarked on her writing in stages under the guidance of Father Gamard, who in the reading found her words and interpretation of doctrine transforming and elevating. As Marie-Aimée had only an hour a day available to work on her treatise, it took her five years to complete, during which time she suffered much community suspicion, personal doubts and bodily afflictions, exacerbated by the election of Sister Isabelle as prioress. But Marie-Aimée endured all this and persistently continued to make herself available to receive divine wisdom. She consulted very few intellectual works during her research, allowing herself instead to be led and instructed solely by the Lord.[8]

When Father Gamard was transferred from Paris, he and the young nun kept in touch through correspondence. The priest asked her to write an account of the graces God had bestowed on her, which she did alongside her other work. At the outbreak of the Franco-Prussian war of 1870, her 'imperturbable interior peace' provided an outer confidence and security against any threats. At her suggestion, the 'monastic family secured the special protection of heaven through a vow'.

During the final years of her life, Marie-Aimée became a decisive and energetic novice mistress, sharing 'the supernatural illuminations' she received for the good of the souls under her care. One postulant recalled encountering her saintliness at the grille: 'She looked at me gently and said a few words but how much this look taught me.'

Yet Marie-Aimée continued to suffer suspicion from various clergy. She had already destroyed 'voluminous notes on the Song of Songs to protect herself from being misunderstood' and, like Saint Bernadette of Lourdes after her (whose dates of life, 1844–79, closely overlapped Marie-Aimée's),[9] she had to endure being questioned and investigated by church authorities over the authenticity of the mysteries revealed to her, up to the time of her death.

After contracting pleurisy, Sister Marie-Aimée wrote a summation of the state of her soul (using the third-person narrative), which she intended for Father Gamard. It reflects the completion of a unique journey to perfection, rarely recounted. It shows the ascent of a soul from all base desires, all vice, all imperfections. It exposes a spirit free of worldly attachments, of ego, of the burdens of humanity, who was ready, like a bird, to soar to the light, clear in her knowledge of whom she belonged to and where she was going.

> *This soul forgets everything: she is like an alien. She no longer petitions for herself, but the Holy Spirit inspires her with prayers that completely correspond to her requirements and are of great perfection… This soul is at peace. For the most part, she does not dwell on the graces she used to receive and cannot even do so… If she must write about them, she does so immediately and limits herself to important aspects that especially occur to her and whose communication she sees will serve the glory of God or the salvation of souls… This soul no longer considers herself superior to others and judges nothing. She disclaims herself and esteems others very highly… She no longer knows hypocrisy, but is as simple as a child… She desires for herself and in everything only the fulfilment of what pleases God. She desires no more talent, graces, or holiness than God has decided to give to her. Indeed she has an unquenchable thirst for suffering and humiliation, but still she wants only what God wants… She turns naturally to Jesus as if he alone existed. And since he always answers her, she forgets more and more all that is created and depends on her dearly beloved alone. She is free, nothing disconcerts her. She is ready to obey anyone… Looking at her failures does not disconcert her, and she seldom notices those of others and always forgives them.*

A year after the birth of another great Carmelite—Saint Thérèse of Lisieux—on the morning of 4 May 1874, Sister

Marie-Aimée de Jésus turned her eyes to heaven, smiled with happiness and then, with 'surprise and delight', raised herself up to pass over to her Lord. As she had written in a hymn of thanksgiving:

My dearly beloved has taken me from myself to become more his own! I am the prey of his love! He is in me like a fiery torrent, sweeping my soul into the sea of endless love, into God.

SPIRITUAL SUMMATION

The prayer of becoming so loved as to be swept into God's endlessness seems a far-reaching desire, but Marie-Aimée achieved that end. She systematically purged herself from all that separated her, all that caused her suffering, to enable her transformation into that loving union.

Much of Marie-Aimée's spirituality, like that of so many Carmelites, was influenced by the writings and teachings of Saint John of the Cross. His contribution to inviting desire and directing the progress to divine unity has always been an indispensable resource. Marie-Aimée had recorded details in her writings of a retreat she took in 1871[10] on Saint John of the Cross's *The Ascent of Mount Carmel*, a treatise described by a recent editor of his work as 'how to reach divine union quickly'.[11] Within this work, Saint John of the Cross provided a verse that augments the message in John's Gospel. The life to be lost is the *sense* of self—and all aspects of that sensed self—as independent and separate from God. Unity is fulfilled only when one is empty of all attachments to desires—even non-desires—within oneself. Saint John of the Cross pointed to the blatant nakedness of sensory purgation that reaches its fulfilment through the following words:

> *To reach satisfaction in all*
> *desire satisfaction in nothing.*
> *To come to possess all*
> *desire to possess nothing.*
> *To arrive at being all*
> *desire to be nothing.*
> *To come to the knowledge of all*
> *desire the knowledge of nothing.*[12]

'In this nakedness,' Saint John wrote, 'the spirit finds its quietude and rest.'[13]

Marie-Aimée's degrees of silence lead to the same end as Saint John's: the twelfth degree is to present oneself 'exposed' and 'nothing' in front of God. What differentiates Saint John's and Marie-Aimée's contributions to this common end is that his defines the rule, whereas hers provides the directions. The Twelve Degrees of Silence point to the stages a person needs to undergo to bring 'Jesus to life'[14] within and slowly be transformed to the place where 'there will be nothing left but Christ'.[15]

The discipline that Marie-Aimée applies towards divine unity is not solely a system of purgation to be undertaken through will alone. It is love that she emphasises over and again, that drives her towards this nakedness, this nothingness. She wrote that her life 'is love and love is union'.[16] Her purpose (defined by our Lord in mutual conversation) was to 'cast her nets' and advance on to high waters, where she would be 'free of everything and of herself'.[17] For Marie-Aimée knew that taking the path of love meant unity, and to come to unity meant purification and transformation from all that could hinder such an outcome. She heard from her Lord that the soul can be made compliant only when it is 'void of preferences, personal will, attachments and desires', if she 'renders herself entirely to me through organising the degrees by which she is to be elevated'.[18]

For Marie-Aimée, this transformation was to arrive at being 'nothing at all, nothing, nothing, nothing',[19] so as to become 'the most pure temple' where 'there exists no noise, all is silent, peaceful and contemplative', where her heart is the sanctuary and she lives 'only God's life'.[20] Marie-Aimée experienced that which the apostle Paul described: she was alive only to God, and it was Christ who lived in her (Galatians 2:19–20). She had received the rewards of surrendering all to her Lord, and, in the joy of such a state, she found the freedom and love to exclaim, in the end, that she had become 'a pure current that flows in God, into the torrent dissolved without trace'.[21]

Saint John of the Cross used a different analogy for the same end. He wrote, 'For the soul united and transformed in God breathes out God to God the very divine aspiration that God... breathes out in himself to her.[22]

Praying the Twelve Degrees of Silence

Who are you, sweet light, that fills me
And illumines the darkness of my heart?
You lead me like a mother's hand,
And should you let go of me,
I would not know how to take another step.
You are the space
That embraces my being and buries it in yourself
Away from you it sinks into the abyss
Of nothingness, from which you raised it to the light.
You, nearer to me than I to myself
And more interior than my most interior
And still impalpable and intangible
And beyond any name
Holy Spirit—eternal love.

EDITH STEIN [23]

There exists no formal methodology for praying with the Twelve Degrees of Silence, but the degrees themselves, by their very nature, fall into four specific groups. Within her text, Marie-Aimée guides the first three degrees as preparation to becoming 'the silent servant of Divine Love' (No. 3). The next three open one to hear 'the first note of the sacred song, the song of the heavens' (No. 6). The following three are aids in perfecting a simple purity, considered as 'blessed childhood' (No. 9), and the last three as preparing and experiencing the gift of silence as an eternal state of unity (No. 12). These four themes, in groupings of three, can provide guidance for the particular spiritual intent of the degrees and for where each one, sequentially, is leading.

Commitment is key to being guided by the degrees of silence as a daily practice of prayerful awareness. A desire to learn by experiencing what they can teach is an imperative, as is a sincere readiness to be changed in the process. As Edith Stein instructed:

Human beings are called to live in their inmost region and to have themselves as much in hand as is possible from that centrepoint; only from there can they rightly come to terms with the world. Only from there can they find the place in the world that has been intended for them.[24]

Finding one's place in the world through contemplation points to an alternative way to wilful seeking and personal planning. Journeying to the interior of Self requires silence to discover the hidden treasures within. Regular and ordered reflection time, put aside for this very purpose, will eventually reveal the rewards of clarity, revelation, truth and love.

Listening as prayer calls for receptive devotion. Beginning each day in silence, aware of the presence of God in the heart through meditation and a quiet time reading daily scripture (*lectio divina*), including The Twelve Degrees of Silence, beautifully complements such prayer that draws you closer to God.

You may wish to concentrate on one degree per month, in order that it can permeate its wisdom as the process delicately unfolds. How much time to take with each degree is purely a personal preference, but following them in sequence is essential.

Once you have begun, making an intention before the active day begins to apply the teachings of each assigned degree can help bring them alive in attitude. During evening prayer, you can monitor your progress as part of the day's examination of conscience. Questions and reflections to guide this examination accompany each degree.

Keeping a journal helps chart your soul's growth and enables you to note what needs, or continues to need, attention.

After completing the practicum of the entire twelve degrees, you can keep them alive as daily companions and reminders of what you still need to work on as well as what you can celebrate as successful.

May Marie-Aimée de Jésus' degrees of silence provide a seedbed for God to create within you and bring forth the grace to embrace a constant intimate encounter with the eternal love of the Creator through our Lord Jesus Christ.

The Twelve Degrees of Silence by Marie-Aimée de Jésus

Additional reflections by Lucinda M. Vardey

The interior life
1. Silence in words
2. Silence in actions
3. Silence with one's imagination
4. Silence with one's memories
5. Silence with others
6. Silence with one's heart
7. Silence to self-interest
8. Silence of the mind
9. Silence to judgements
10. Silence to the will
11. Silence towards oneself
12. Silence with God

The interior life

There is no other word that singularly summarises the distinct quality of interior life than silence. To embrace silence is to prepare for holiness. Silence is the company on the path.

God, who is eternal, speaks only one Word.

It would be desirable to speak in correspondence with God.

All our words, directly or indirectly, should express Jesus.

How beautiful is the language of silence!

Silence in words

The first indispensable step towards divine union requires a practice of speaking less to the created and much to the Creator.

It is within this school of solitude and silence that the rudimentary principles are revealed. In the spirit of the Gospel and the Rule [the Carmelite Rule of Life] which the soul has embraced, the soul learns and deepens in virtue and respect. Respect is given to the consecrated holy places, extended towards others, and most of all to the Word that rests in the bosom of the Father, the Word made flesh.

Not listening to the world and its news allows space to be silent with God, to listen only to God's voice and the voices of the holiest of souls. It is to be as silent as Mary, who was able to hear the voice of the angel.

1: GUIDED REFLECTION

**Set a guard over my mouth, O Lord;
keep watch over the door of my lips.**
PSALM 141:3

- Do you really need to speak?
- Do communicating and speaking serve an existing and developing relationship?
- Does every word you share express your heart?
- Is it possible to listen more?
- Are the environments for sharing safe and suitable for abject honesty and truth?
- Is all your conversation founded on mutual respect?
- Do you find opportunities to express yourself silently? (For example, through contemplative and listening prayer, time in nature and with creation, adoration, being quietly present with the troubled, sick and dying)

And what is there on this earth for this soul who, touched by faith, sees through its shadows a superior world on the threshold of eternity?

My God, my God, only you are kind! Leave some moments of silence for my love.

MARIE-AIMÉE DE JÉSUS, *À L'ÉCOLE DE L'AMOUR*

Silence in actions

Silence in the workplace and slowness in our movements. Silence in walking, softness in looking, gentleness in speaking, blocking out all noise. Being silent to everything exterior is a preparation for the soul to pass into God.

From these first efforts, the soul deserves to hear the voice of the Lord. How well these first steps are rewarded! God calls the soul to the desert, which is why the soul avoids every distraction in this second stage. She steps away from noise, runs away alone to the One who is alone.

There she will taste the first taste of divine union and savour the jealousy of her God. This is the silence of contemplation.

2: GUIDED REFLECTION

Be still, and know that I am God!
PSALM 46:10

- Where can gentleness find expression in your every day?
- What is required for you to be more gentle with yourself?
- Are there incidents of hurry and hardness in your life that need transforming?
- How comfortable—or uncomfortable—is silence for you?
- What distractions keep you from being silent? Are these distractions exterior or interior or both?
- Can you put aside 2.4 hours a day (one-tenth of your day) to be alone with God?
- What changes do you need to make to put aside this time?
- Are your activities propelled by self-desire or prayerful obedience?
- Can your thoughts and activities merge into contemplative gestures?

O my Lord, what shelter have you prepared for a soul so feeble as mine, so that, independent of this incumbent body, she might elevate herself to her Creator and her All?

MARIE-AIMÉE DE JÉSUS, *À L'ÉCOLE DE L'AMOUR*

Silence with one's imagination

The first faculty of imagination—imagining things, imagining God—comes knocking at the closed door of the garden (Song of Songs 5:1–2), bringing with it emotions, vague impressions, fears and sadness. In solitude, the soul stays in silence.

But it is in this secluded place that the soul proves her love of the Beloved.

The soul will then present to the All-Powerful the beauties of the sky, the delights of her Lord, the scenes of Calvary, the perfections of her God.

From remaining in this silence, she becomes the silent servant of divine love.

3. GUIDED REFLECTION

Hope in God; for I shall again praise him.
PSALM 42:5

- How vivid is your imagination?
- How much time in a day do you spend unaware of the present?
- How much acceptance for *what is* can live in your heart?
- Can you release yearnings to understand or work out?
- Do you fill emptiness—interior or exterior—with material satisfactions (such as entertainment or socialising)?
- Do you like being alone? If not, why?
- Is living more simply and quietly an option for you?
- Describe your own garden of Eden.
- How much of this garden is expressed in you?

The closer you come to God, the more you want to get near him. The more you unite with him, the more you desire to be united with him. The more you take part in God, if I can express myself in such a manner, the more you are unquenched.

MARIE-AIMÉE DE JÉSUS, *SUR L'UNION DIVINE ET LA TRANSFORMATION DE L'ÂME EN DIEU*

Silence with one's memories

We need to forget the past.
 In order to do so, we need to saturate our minds with memories of all the good things God has done for us and the mercy God has extended.

Through silence, we recognise the abundance of God and live in a state of gratitude.

4: GUIDED REFLECTION

> I will bless the Lord at all times:
> his praise shall continually be in my mouth.
> PSALM 34:1

- How much of the past affects your present?
- What hurts, disappointments and regrets do you carry in your heart? (List them.)
- Make a list of the prominent gifts you have received as evidence of God's generosity.
- Write a prayer of penance and a prayer of thanksgiving from these lists.
- Consider ways in which you can find closure for past hurts, disappointments and regrets.
- Consider what is required to embrace 'a gratitude attitude', especially in prayer.

Silence with others

How miserable is this habitual condition! Often, while meditating, the soul catches herself interiorly conversing with others, talking and answering them. To persist in this manner causes humiliation and provokes the saints to mourn!

Under such circumstances, the soul must gently retire to the most intimate depths of herself, where rests the inaccessible majesty of the Holy of Holies; where Jesus, her consoler and her God, will reveal himself to her and disclose his secrets. He will give her a foretaste of bliss.

Then Jesus will give her a bitter distaste for all that is not him, and all that is of the earth and the world will cease, little by little, to distract her.

5: GUIDED REFLECTION

For God alone my soul waits in silence.
PSALM 62:5

- Do the people in your life disturb or comfort and complement you?
- Do you allow others' ways to affect your way of being?
- Do you often spend time rehearsing what to say or how to be in relationship, or mulling over, after the fact, what was said and done?
- Do the actions—or inactions—of others disappoint you?
- Can you try not to care about being cared for by others, but only by God?
- How intimate and constant is your relationship with Jesus?

I am not attached: what I mean to say is that I have no unregulated affections—to my country, nor the cell I occupy, or the habit I wear, nor to whomever or whatever. I feel ready to go anywhere God bids me —in life or death.
MARIE-AIMÉE DE JÉSUS, *SUR L'UNION DIVINE ET LA TRANSFORMATION DE L'ÂME EN DIEU*

Silence with one's heart

With the tongue mute, the senses calm, one's imagination, memories and other things all brought to silence, comes solitude. Solitude breeds a purity of soul similar to that of a spiritual bride. The heart makes little noise.

We have to be silent to our affections, our antipathies, our desires, especially when they are overly ardent. We have to be silent to zeal when it becomes indiscreet, silent to fervour when it is exaggerated. Even a whisper needs to be silent.

We have to be silent to the excitement of love, but we mustn't be silent to holy exultations of which God is the author.

We don't say 'no' to the love of God, but we say 'no' to the more basic human expressions of desire.

The silence of love is love in silence. Silence in the presence of God, who is beauty, kindness and perfection.

Silence with one's heart is beyond words. It is a silence that is not forced or awkward; it naturally *is*. It is a silence that will not harm tenderness. Vigour of love for God, as an admission of all that is false, will not harm the silence of the humble. As angels' wings flutter, of which spoke the prophet,[25] the sound of their wings does not harm the silence of their obedience, as the *fiat* of the Virgin Mary ('Let it be to me...') does not harm the silence of Gethsemane, nor does the eternal *Sanctus* harm the silence of the seraphim.

A silent heart is a pure heart; a melody singing in the heart of God. Like a sacristy lamp flickering noiselessly at the tabernacle, and like incense silently rising at the Saviour's throne, such is love's silence.

In the preceding degrees (Nos. 1–5), silence was a cry of the earth. In this degree (No. 6), the soul, in her purity, learns the first note of the sacred song, the song of the heavens.

6: GUIDED REFLECTION

Let my prayer be counted as incense before you.
PSALM 141:2

- Does peace constantly reside within you?
- How much more solitude can you introduce into your life?
- Is the middle way a path you frequent?
- Is there a balance now between your interior and exterior life?
- Does inner peace stay with you when you are outside?
- Are you confident in being able to discern where it is inappropriate to be involved?
- Is saying 'No' to that which is inappropriate difficult or easy for you?
- Is silence becoming more familiar in prayer for you?
- Do you treasure silence as vital?
- Are you letting God act more freely within you?
- How are you experiencing God's presence within?
- How central is your heart in prayer?
- How much love are you bringing to your growing relationship with Jesus within?
- Are you aware of any impurities in your heart?
- How is your practice of patience?

I want to sing a song for you composed of whispers in memory of your blessedness and my faults.

MARIE-AIMÉE DE JÉSUS, *À L'ÉCOLE DE L'AMOUR*

7

Silence to self-interest

A love of self is easily tempted to corrupt. Silence resists such lures. Silence prevents the soul from low-level inclinations.

Through gentleness and humility bred in silence, one is able to detach from all negative things, including contemptuous accusations or malicious gossip. However, one also needs to be not only deaf to the negative but also to the positive, to acknowledgements, compliments and approval.

The soul stays in constant gentleness and humility, steadily silent in pleasure and joy. Just as a flower unfolds in silence and its scent worships its Creator in silence, the interior soul must do likewise. She needs to be silent in the face of contradictions, in fasting, during sleeplessness at night, in fatigue and in hot and cold temperatures. Silence in health and in illness, in deprivations of all kinds. Silence speaks most eloquently from true poverty and penance. This silence is made comfortable when it is dead towards all that the world offers.

Detachment breaks the bond of material enslavement. It is the silence of the human self passing into the will of God. Unsteady human nature cannot interrupt this silence, because it is a silence that stretches beyond ourselves and our natural tendencies.

7: GUIDED REFLECTION

Lead me to the rock that is higher than I.
PSALM 61:2

- Is self-focus painful or pleasurable for you?
- Do you seek for God alone and God's will?
- How much freedom lives within you?
- Is the realm of God and the communion of saints as familiar to you as family?
- Has detachment from yourself and others become a constant reality?
- Are you feeling surer of the steadfast love of God?
- Do you follow the inner promptings of the wisdom of God without fail?

The spiritual understanding of death within transformation does not mean physically dying but living life hidden in God with Jesus Christ.

MARIE-AIMÉE DE JÉSUS, *LA VIERGE FÉCONDE*

Silence of the mind

The way silence influences the workings of the mind is to disable useless thoughts, agreeable thoughts and natural thoughts. Even though a thought itself cannot help its thinking, these three thoughts are the ones that harm the silence of the mind.

The Twelve Degrees of Silence

Our minds desire truth, yet we feed our minds lies. The essential truth is God. God's intelligence is limitless and ours is limited. Because of our limitations, we are not able to contemplate God consistently—and access God's wisdom in the moment—without the generous gift of God's grace. This grace, although impossible to be summoned, can be accessed only through prayer. If you silence your thoughts by means of faith, the result will be partially illuminative.

Try to prevent yourself from working thoughts out intellectually, because by doing so, you weaken your aim and dry up the love in you.

Silence your intentions in purity and simplicity. In solitude, silence obsessive thinking. In meditation, silence curiosity. In devotion, silence personal desires and plans, as they hinder the work of God in you.

Silence pride, which is always looking out for itself in everything, everywhere, searching for sublimity, beauty and goodness. Be silent, instead, in the naked, radical honesty of a saint's simplicity.

A mind that fights against all such enemies is similar to angels who look ceaselessly upon the face of God. It is only through this kind of intelligence that one is raised nearer to God.

8: GUIDED REFLECTION

Look to him, and be radiant.
PSALM 34:5

- Consider monitoring your thoughts by counting their frequency and their themes.
- Find ways in which to redirect your mind, such as meditation and solitude.
- Spend more time with scripture through *lectio divina* and other holy reading to focus an inquisitive mind.
- Disable excessive stimulation.
- Seek a more child-like attitude.
- Turn your inward gaze towards the face of God.

How much light is poured from this obscure faith into a well-disposed mind, a mind completely devoid of its own knowledge.

MARIE-AIMÉE DE JÉSUS, *SUR L'UNION DIVINE ET LA TRANSFORMATION DE L'ÂME EN DIEU*

Silence to judgements

Abstain from judging people and things.
Do not judge or pass an opinion. By saying nothing, you must not surrender to that which is morally wrong. When you speak, do so simply from the heart, with prudence and kindness.

It is as the silence of blessed childhood, the silence of perfection.

It is as the silence of angels and archangels as they follow the commandments of God.

It is as the silence of the Word made flesh.

9: GUIDED REFLECTION

I am silent; I do not open my mouth.
PSALM 39:9

- Notice when you assume a position and let it go.
- Become aware of when you separate yourself from God, others and the environment.
- Put your mind where your heart is.
- Follow your heart in determining the right thing to do or not to do.
- Listen to God for all direction.
- Let silence determine the right outcome.

All faults, even the smallest ones, are consequences of bad habits.

MARIE-AIMÉE DE JÉSUS, *SUR L'UNION DIVINE ET LA TRANSFORMATION DE L'ÂME EN DIEU*

10

Silence to the will

Adherence to the commandments and the sacred Rule [the Rule of the convent] requires a type of silence that is exterior to one's own will.

Here the Lord introduces a much more profound and difficult teaching. It is the silence of a slave receiving blows from its master. Blessed is this slave because its master is God!

This is the silence surrounding the victim on the altar, the silence of the lamb that has been sheared. It is the silence of darkness that prohibits our calling out for light, the divine light that brings happiness.

It is the silence of an anxious heart, a suffering soul, who thought herself loved by her God. Pushed away, she doesn't ask why or how long she will suffer. It is the silence of abandonment where she experiences God's unyielding severity. It is the silence of heaviness under the weight of the divine hand.

It is the silence that makes no sound except the sound of suffering love. It is the silence of the cross. It is more than a martyr's silence: it is the silence of Jesus' agony. This silence is his divine silence: there is nothing like his voice; it is impossible to resist his prayer. Nothing is more worthy of God than this kind of suffering praise. Just as Mary's 'Yes' included the embrace of pain, this silence allies us with the birth pangs of death.

While the human will suffers through the emptiness of abandonment, which is the true sacrifice of love, it is violently tossed like great waves upon rocks for the glory of God's name. God is transforming the human will into his divine will.

What now is incomplete? What more is needed to accomplish divine union? What will it take to achieve the splendour of Christ in the soul?

The answer is twofold: (1) the body's last breath, and (2) the sweet attentiveness to the Beloved, whose divine kiss is the reward beyond description.

10: GUIDED REFLECTION

Be still before the Lord, and wait patiently for him.
PSALM 37:7

- The way of the cross was imbued with redemptive silence. To align one's whole self to the will of God requires purgative suffering. This can take many forms. Suffering is not wasted if it is made prayerful and offered as an oblation or gift to God.
- How is the process of dying to self unfolding in you?
- What percentage of trust are you according God in the process?
- Are you able to fully embrace the idea that all that is given is from God's love?
- Can you be satisfied with and in God alone?

My will is still weak on occasion. I too easily fall prey to the delusion that what I consider to be God's will is, in fact, my own.

MARIE-AIMÉE DE JÉSUS, *SUR L'UNION DIVINE ET LA TRANSFORMATION DE L'ÂME EN DIEU*

11
Silence towards oneself

Prevent talking to yourself and carrying on interior conversations.
Do not listen to yourself.
Do not complain.
Do not feel sorry for yourself.
In brief: silence yourself.
Forget yourself.
Separate yourself from yourself.

This is the most difficult of silences. Yet silence towards oneself is essential. There is no other way to unite to God as perfectly as is possible. Although, with the aid of grace, a poor little creature can often reach this level, it is especially hard to maintain.

The silence of being nothing is more heroic than the silence of death.

11: GUIDED REFLECTION

You are my Lord; I have no good apart from you.
PSALM 16:2

- How are the virtues of patience and humility revealing themselves to you?
- Can you transcend self-identification (such as name, culture, work, accomplishments and reputation) and self-individuation (such as personality, preferences, emotions and desires)?
- Can you silence self-concern?
- Can you detach from involvement and become a witness to yourself and others?
- Can you belong solely to God?

Her interior eye is always fixed on me, freely responding to even the smallest signs, fleeing from her nature and isolating herself from her volition. Her heart guesses and anticipates my desires: she runs after the more perfect desire and embraces it with love for love of me.

THE LORD IN CONVERSATION WITH MARIE-AIMÉE'S SOUL, *Á L'ÉCOLE DE L'AMOUR*

12

Silence with God

In the beginning, God said to the soul, 'Don't speak too much to others, but speak a lot to me.' Now God says to the soul, 'Don't talk to me any more.'

Silence with God is to be united with God—to present oneself, exposed, in front of God, to offer oneself to God, to become nothing in front of God; adore God, love God, listen to God, hear God and find rest in God.

It is the silence of eternity that unites the soul with God.

12: GUIDED REFLECTION

Happy are all who take refuge in him.
PSALM 2:11

- Can you pray without words?
- Can you relax with God as you truly are?
- Is there anything that prevents you from achieving intimacy with God?
- Does the silence of God live inside you as indwelling light?
- Can you trust God implicitly for everything?
- Are you afraid to die?
- Do you experience the joy of the Lord's abiding?
- Is there anything else you desire?

Such is the enormous generosity of this soul who grants me all the glory that is due me. In her purity, transfigured and absorbed into God, she lives only God's life.

THE LORD SPEAKING TO MARIE-AIMÉE'S SOUL, *À L'ÉCOLE DE L'AMOUR*

Afterword: Only God's life

In her purity, transfigured and absorbed in God, she lives only God's life.[26]

A pilgrim sets off to an unknown destination. There's trust, however, that much will be in store, because those who have taken the journey before have been transformed from who they were on departure to who they were to become in the wholeness and fullness of God. On the way there is shedding and leaving behind, and dust to be shaken off the feet. Whatever happens, the assurance that all will certainly be better than it was, that the rewards and treasures are indeed worth the toil, is what draws us to journey.

The journey is a solitary one, as each soul is called by name. The call is to an intimate encounter with the One who supplies everything, a growing relationship with the One who guides everything, a trusting confidence that all is already within us and will be exposed in its appropriate time. We learn to open ourselves to *receive* what we need, to be conscious of and cooperate with the changes we must make, to be aware of what separates us from the measure of God's love.

Jesus, who desires to make a home in us, to dwell within, to inform our every step, to bring us eventually the joy of being at home *in* him, walks the kenotic (self-emptying) way. To follow him personally is to be like the seed that dies into the earth of his divinity, allowing him the space and capacity to blossom within us. A new flower then grows, nourished daily by the waters of grace as it keeps its face illumined by the light of his magnificence.

> *From this moment onward I go forward*
> *into the fullness beyond time, and there, where time rests*
> *in the stillness of Eternity, I will repose in silence.*
> THE GOSPEL OF MARY (MAGDALA), DIALOGUE 4[27]

Notes

1 From Simone Weil, *Waiting on God* trans. Emma Crauford (Fount, 1977), p. 134.
2 See Revelation 3:20.
3 Edith Stein, *The Science of the Cross*, Josephine Koeppel OCD, trans. (ICS, 2002), p. 55.
4 See Thomas Merton, *Thoughts in Solitude* (Shambhala, 1993), p. 130.
5 Saint John of the Cross, 'The Living Flame of Love', in *The Collected Works of St John of the Cross*, Kieran Kavanaugh OCD and Otilio Rodriguez OCD, trans. (ICS1991), p. 644.
6 Non-annotated quotes are taken from Edith Stein, '11.4 A chosen vessel of divine wisdom: Sr Marie-Aimée de Jésus of the Carmel of the Avenue de Saxe in Paris 1839–1874', trans. Waltraut Stein, in *The Hidden Life: Vol. 4 of the Collected Works of Edith Stein* (ICS, 1992), pp. 76–90, and Marie-Aimée de Jésus, *À l'École de l'Amour* (*At the School of Love*), *La Vierge Féconde* (*The Fertile Virgin*), *Sur l'Union Divine et la Transformation de l'Âme en Dieu* (*On Divine Union and the Transformation of the Soul in God*), and *La Vie Cachée en Dieu* (*The Hidden Life in God*), in *Les Douze Degrés du Silence* (Arfuyen, 2005) (Françoise Reuter and Lucinda M. Vardey, trans.).
7 Saint Ambrose, quoted in Edith Stein, *Science of the Cross*, p. 63.
8 Marie-Aimée's book in response to Renan's work has been published only in French. The last edition, dated 1974, is out of print.
9 Saint Bernadette Soubirous (7 January 1844–16 April 1879).
10 Marie-Aimée de Jésus, *Sur l'Union Divine et la Transformation de l'Âme en Dieu*, pp. 115–144.
11 Saint John of the Cross, 'The Ascent of Mount Carmel: Prologue', in *The Collected Works of St John of the Cross*, p. 113.

12 Ibid., p. 150.
13 Ibid., p. 151.
14 Marie-Aimée de Jésus, *La Vierge Féconde*, pp. 101–110.
15 Ibid.
16 Marie-Aimée de Jésus, *À l'École de l'Amour*, pp. 75–97.
17 Ibid.
18 Ibid.
19 Ibid.
20 Ibid.
21 Marie-Aimée de Jésus, *La Vie Cachée en Dieu*, p. 148.
22 Saint John of the Cross, 'The Spiritual Canticle: Commentary on Stanza 39', in *The Collected Works of St John of the Cross*, p. 623.
23 Edith Stein, 'And I Remain with You', trans. Waltraut Stein, in *Hidden Life*, p. 141.
24 Edith Stein, *Science of the Cross*, p. 160.
25 Although Marie-Aimée did not specifically say which prophet, it was probably Isaiah, who described seraphs (with six wings). See Isaiah 6:1–3.
26 Marie-Aimée de Jésus, *À l'École de l'Amour*, pp. 75–98.
27 This early Christian gnostic text, papyrus of which was discovered in the late 19th century in Akhmin, Upper Egypt, was translated by Lynn Bauman, Ward Bauman and Cynthia Bourgeault. It is quoted in Cynthia Bourgeault, *The Wisdom Jesus* (Shambhala, 2008), p. 83.

All English quotations of additional works of Marie-Aimée de Jésus are translated from the original French by Françoise Reuter and Lucinda M. Vardey.

Lucinda M. Vardey has written on Catholicism and contemporary spirituality with special emphasis on the works and writings of holy women. Her books include the compilation of the international bestseller of Mother Teresa's *A Simple Path*, an anthology of women's prayers entitled *The Flowering of the Soul*, *Travelling with the Saints in Italy: Contemporary pilgrimages on ancient paths*, and, with her husband, John Dalla Costa, *Being Generous: The art of right living*. She is familiar with the beauty and benefits of silence. Her website is www.dallaluce.com.

Françoise Reuter was educated in Dominican and Jesuit schools in Marseille. In 1973, she emigrated to Canada, where she taught at the Toronto French School as well as being a private tutor. She is married to classics scholar and philosopher Mark Reuter and lives a quiet, secluded life of contemplation and study of the sacred.

Also from BRF

Mary

A gospel witness to transfiguration and liberation

Andrew Jones

Mary is arguably the first disciple, and this book explores the different ways she is presented in the Gospels and also in Christian spirituality through history, showing how her significance extends far beyond the Christmas story. As more than just a mother at the manger, Mary can be a pattern for our own discipleship. She is an enduring witness to the central importance of transfiguration and liberation as characteristics of the kingdom of God, which should also be visible in our lives as followers of Jesus today.

ISBN 978 1 84101 651 1   £8.99
Available from your local Christian bookshop or direct from BRF: please visit www.brfonline.org.uk

Also from BRF

Transformed by the Beloved

A guide to spiritual formation with St John of the Cross

Daniel Muñoz

The 16th-century Spanish mystic John of the Cross is best-known for his reflections on 'the dark night of the soul'. This book explores the dramatic events of his life and times, and also his complex and lyrical poetry, showing how all his work pointed to the reality of God's work through him and presence with him.

Transformed by the Beloved invites us to reflect on different aspects of the Christian journey, all of which John considered crucial for growth in faith and depth of spirituality. Each chapter ends with suggestions for personal reflection and prayer, with many links to John's poems, new translations of which are included in the book.

ISBN 978 1 84101 584 2   £6.99
Available from your local Christian bookshop or direct from BRF: please visit www.brfonline.org.uk

Enjoyed this book?

Write a review—we'd love to hear what you think.
Email: reviews@brf.org.uk

Keep up to date—receive details of our new books as they happen.
Sign up for email news and select your interest groups at:
www.brfonline.org.uk/findoutmore/

Follow us on Twitter @brfonline

By post—to receive new title information by post (UK only), complete the form below and post to: BRF Mailing Lists, 15 The Chambers, Vineyard, Abingdon, Oxfordshire, OX14 3FE

Your Details
Name _____
Address _____
_____
Town/City _____ Post Code _____
Email _____

Your Interest Groups (*Please tick as appropriate)
☐ Advent/Lent ☐ Messy Church
☐ Bible Reading & Study ☐ Pastoral
☐ Children's Books ☐ Prayer & Spirituality
☐ Discipleship ☐ Resources for Children's Church
☐ Leadership ☐ Resources for Schools

Support your local bookshop
Ask about their new title information schemes.